SEO Content Writing 101 For Bloggers

Roggie Clark

Copyright

Title: SEO Content Writing 101 For Bloggers

Author: Roggie Clark

Disclaimer

The views and opinions expressed in this book are those of the author and do not necessarily reflect the official policy or position of any individual, company, or organization cited or referenced in the text. The author is not affiliated with any of the individuals, companies, or organizations mentioned in the text, nor does the author receive any form of compensation for citing or referencing them. Some sample scenarios in this text are fictitious. Any similarity to actual persons, living or dead, is coincidental.

The professional information (strategies, tips, and concepts) in this text is distributed on an "as is" basis, without warranty. While every precaution has been taken in the preparation of the text to ensure all information is accurate, neither the author nor the publisher shall have any liability to any person or entity with respect to any loss or damage caused or alleged to be caused directly or indirectly by the instructions contained in this text or by the computer software and hardware products described in it.

Neither the author nor the publisher guarantees any specific results or outcomes, and the information provided in this text should not be construed as professional advice. Readers should always consult with a qualified professional before making any significant changes to their website or business.

By reading this text, you agree that the author nor the publisher is responsible for any direct, indirect, incidental, or consequential damages that may arise from the use of the information provided. You assume full responsibility for any actions taken based on the information presented in this text.

Table Of Contents

Introduction

When it comes to getting your website's content found online, it is becoming increasingly important for you as a writer to pay attention to SEO or Search Engine Optimization. SEO is becoming more critical whether you are a journalist, content creator, blogger, or business owner, and I'll tell you why.

The reason is the internet is becoming more and more saturated, with thousands of new websites and blogs being created every day. Because of this, "search engines" like Google, Bing, Yahoo!, DuckDuckGo, and others are becoming more and more picky about what content they will and <u>will not</u> include in their indices (online libraries).

So in other words, if your content is not properly "optimized", and engaging there is little to no chance that anyone will stumble upon it on the search results.

This is why so many beginning writers get a "culture shock" when they start blogging on the internet for the first time. Because they are often more accustomed to "traditional writing" like print publications, books, and other scholarly purposes, therefor they neglect SEO and assume that their content will automatically be found and enjoyed by the masses. Unfortunately, this is not the case.

To be successful in this digital age, you need to have a strategy for how to get your content found online, and that is where SEO comes into play.

In this book, I will teach you everything you need to know as a beginner on writing SEO content that you can guarantee will be searchable, engaging, and likely to be shared by your readers.

To do this, I will walk you through my personal process for creating SEO content for my clients. I have broken down this process into three easy-to-follow steps so that you can follow along with them. Then once you have the basics you should start creating your own SEO content.

With that being said, let's get into chapter 1. In this chapter, I discuss what SEO content writing is in a nutshell, and what are the basic components of it.

Chapter 1: SEO Content Writing Basics

While content writing in SEO is about ranking on search engines, it's actually more important that the content be useful to people rather than made just to rank on search engines. The truth is SEO content writing is more about making your content:

- Easier to read
- Easier to share
- Easier to remember

That's it - FOR PEOPLE TO READ - it's just a bonus that search engines may prefer your content over the competition. This is why search engines like Google say in their article ("Creating Helpful, Reliable, People-First Content") that you should create "People-First Content" or content that is written for humans and not for search engines - in other words; write for your audience, not just to rank.

At the end of the day, the only people that really matter are the ones that are reading your content. If you can't engage them with your content, then you are just wasting your time stressing about ranking for whatever topic or *keyword* you might be targeting because you will never rank for it anyway.

I am not being morbid, or melancholy, I have to say this because too many newbs fall into the trap of just spamming their articles with keywords and links thinking that this is what they need to get results. I can always tell when a client has tried their own "magic" or they have an agency working on their account performing "secret sauce".

Which as I said earlier, is usually just spamming the same keyword over and over again, but additionally it has also become the overuse of AI content writers.

This might have worked in the past, back when search engines were more archaic but now they have *NLP (Natural Language Processing)*, and *semantic search.* So they are more privy to related terms, and synonyms of your keywords. So essentially, they know if a bot wrote your content or not.

So to sum up to you all in a nutshell, optimizing your content to SEO best practices is more about making your content more useful and accessible to your audience, and in theory, you can increase the likelihood of ranking higher on search engines. Got it?

Last Thoughts

In my opinion, you shouldn't be spinning your wheels trying to adhere to every new SEO tip or tactic you hear about because the truth is search engines are always changing their algorithms (because again, they follow the people, not the other way around), so a tactic that works today might not work tomorrow. Again, this is why AI content has quickly lost traction, even with minor algorithm updates by search engines.

What's more important is that you have a long-term strategy or process that is focused on producing consistently high-quality content for your audience, with SEO just as the "fuel" to get it in front of the right people.

So with that being said, let's get into chapter 2 and that is, what in my opinion the SEO content writing process should include.

Chapter 2: My SEO Content Writing Process Explained

You will definitely hear other SEO professionals or even AI apps mention that SEO content writing is about "keyword density", "content-length", "having a fast website", and "having a bunch of pictures, and infographics". Yes, these things matter, in context, but they are not hard fast rules, they're just "tactics" that really don't have any concrete data behind them or well-established consensus.

Every pro is different, but with me, when it comes to writing for SEO, my process only consists of three things:

1. **Finding a topic**
2. **Making the content searchable**
3. **Sharing it with relevant people**

In each of these steps, there are SEO concepts weaved in there, but not in a way that is overly technical and full of tactics that are really not that important anyway.

Here's what I mean; **Step 1. Finding a searchable topic**: This is all about choosing the right *keywords* and finding relevant topics and themes that your core audience is searching for. **Step 2. Making the content easy to read and understand**: this is about using *On-Page SEO* (we will discuss this later) to help make the content easier to engage with and also readable for search engines, **Step 3. Sharing it with relevant people**: this last step is all about getting other websites to share and talk about your articles. This process is also referred to as *Link-Building.* '

Let me give you a quick crash course on each of these SEO concepts. It will help you better understand my process.

SEO Concepts Explained

- **Keyword Research:** involves identifying the words and phrases i.e. "*keywords*" that readers use when searching for articles, products, or services similar to what your website offers. So you can include them in your own content to help it become more searchable.

- **On-Page SEO:** generally refers to optimizing the user-facing elements on a webpage that provide basic information about the article, like the title (Title tag), description on what it is about (Meta description), headings etc.

- **Link-Building:** refers to getting "backlinks" or other websites to share your articles, additionally, it helps search engines see you as a more credible source, and thus they may recommend you more.

As you can see, my process is just basic SEO concepts with all the jargon, tactics, and whimsical ideas left out. I did it like this because I honestly wish someone had done it for me. Wasting your time with silly SEO tactics is a cat-and-mouse game where you never know what the search engines will do next. So what may get you results today, will be obsolete tomorrow.

So again, it's better to focus on mastering concepts rather than tactics. But I know a lot of readers are hard-headed so let me tell you in more detail why.

Why Do You Recommend Producing Content Like This?

I know you might be thinking to yourself - *"Is that all there is to it?"*. Yes - SEO content writing in my opinion has become too much about trying to "dupe" search engines or trying to overly adhere to SEO suggestions. That it has become too robotic, what I am finding, is that these blogs might rank high on search engines, but they are not necessarily receiving the engagement that they should.

From my own experience, I've found it frustrating to read the content, specifically on recipe blogs, because they have spent so much time trying to implement "SEO tactics" that the readability was left out. Look at this recipe I was checking out on pumpkin cheesecake, shown in the screenshot below. It honestly took me a while to scroll through the entire post just to get to the recipe ingredients:

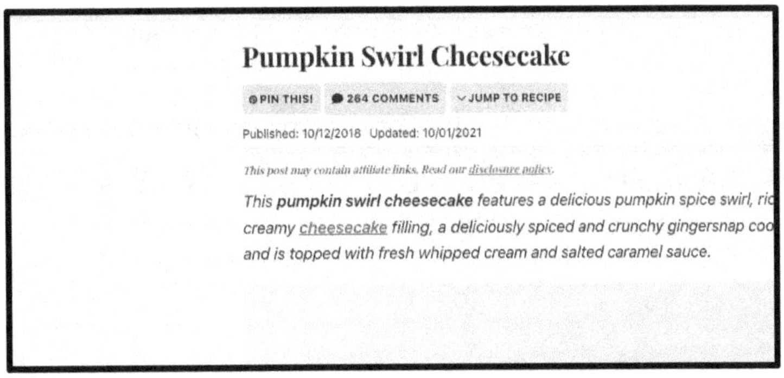

As you can see in the screenshot below it has links to webpages that aren't super relevant to the recipe ("apple cider donuts", "jalapeño bread"), and the link text or "anchor text" looks spammy. Again this is probably fueled by an SEO tactic about using "keywords" or important phrases in your link text to get better rankings.

This is the next scroll, as you can see in the screenshot below, now the blogger is talking about "Tips for making the perfect cheesecake". Great, but couldn't this have been another post, or at the end of the recipe? Again, this tactic is fueled by the belief that you need to have a certain number of words on your webpage. Again, I still haven't reached the ingredients yet.

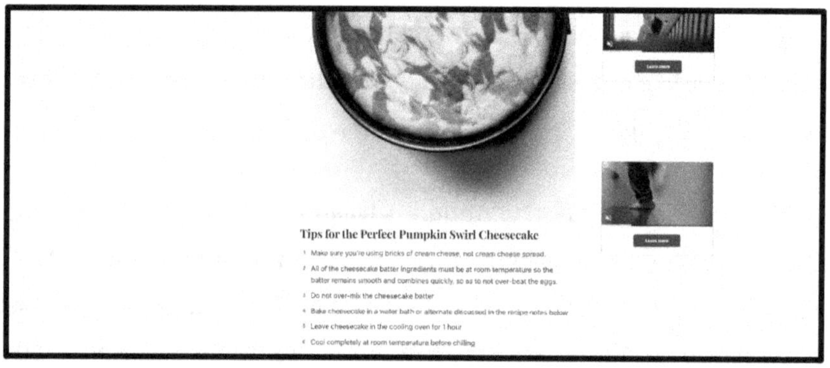

Then this one, "How to freeze cheesecake", is shown in the screenshot below. Again this is great info, but couldn't this have come at the end or in another post?

But again, this tactic is specifically for ranking on Google. This tactic is about looking up your keyword on Google, and then referring to their "People Ask Question" section to find questions that you can answer in your blog post.

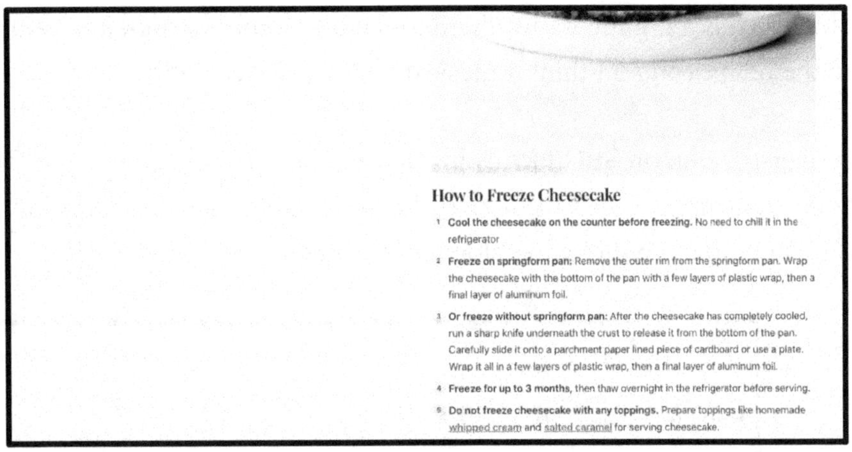

How to Freeze Cheesecake

1. **Cool the cheesecake on the counter before freezing.** No need to chill it in the refrigerator
2. **Freeze on springform pan:** Remove the outer rim from the springform pan. Wrap the cheesecake with the bottom of the pan with a few layers of plastic wrap, then a final layer of aluminum foil.
3. **Or freeze without springform pan:** After the cheesecake has completely cooled, run a sharp knife underneath the crust to release it from the bottom of the pan. Carefully slide it onto a parchment paper lined piece of cardboard or use a plate. Wrap it all in a few layers of plastic wrap, then a final layer of aluminum foil.
4. **Freeze for up to 3 months,** then thaw overnight in the refrigerator before serving.
5. **Do not freeze cheesecake with any toppings.** Prepare toppings like homemade whipped cream and salted caramel for serving cheesecake.

I grabbed a screenshot below. Looky looky the one she addressed in her recipe was similar to a question that was listed! See, I am not making this stuff up! It's like the blogger used a hundred SEO tactics in this one post!

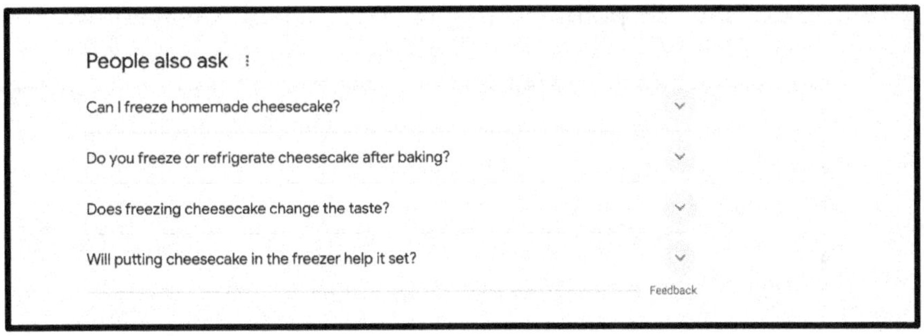

People also ask

Can I freeze homemade cheesecake?

Do you freeze or refrigerate cheesecake after baking?

Does freezing cheesecake change the taste?

Will putting cheesecake in the freezer help it set?

Feedback

Now, after what almost felt like an hour of scrolling, I finally reached the description, with the actual ingredients and the recipe. I am going to be honest, I felt like I was never going to get there!

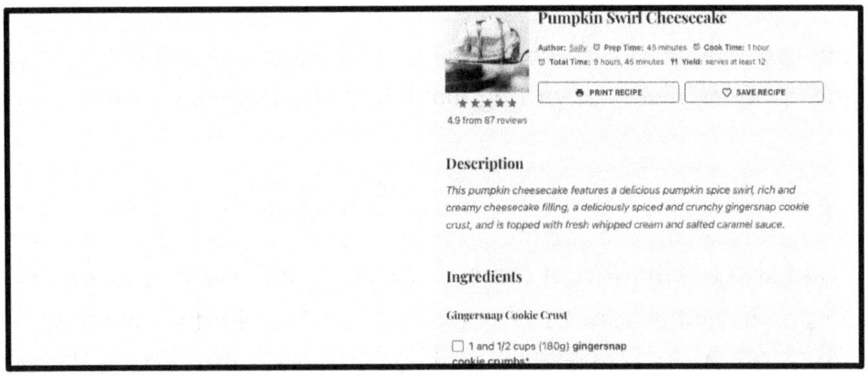

Pumpkin Swirl Cheesecake

Author: Sally Prep Time: 45 minutes Cook Time: 1 hour
Total Time: 9 hours, 45 minutes Yield: serves at least 12

PRINT RECIPE SAVE RECIPE

★★★★★
4.9 from 87 reviews

Description

This pumpkin cheesecake features a delicious pumpkin spice swirl, rich and creamy cheesecake filling, a deliciously spiced and crunchy gingersnap cookie crust, and is topped with fresh whipped cream and salted caramel sauce.

Ingredients

Gingersnap Cookie Crust

- [ ] 1 and 1/2 cups (180g) gingersnap cookie crumbs*

As you can see, this recipe blogger was focusing too much on tactics and not readability. If someone is in the middle of making this cheesecake for instance, and they just need to pull up the recipe quickly, it is a nightmare for them to have to scroll through a page and a half of stuff just to get to the recipe (oh no I think I messed up the cheesecake!).

This over-fixation on SEO tactics just to rank has become a major problem, and it has led to a loss of engagement i.e. a loss of money! Just look at this screenshot below. See I am not the only one who is frustrated with recipe blogs these days:

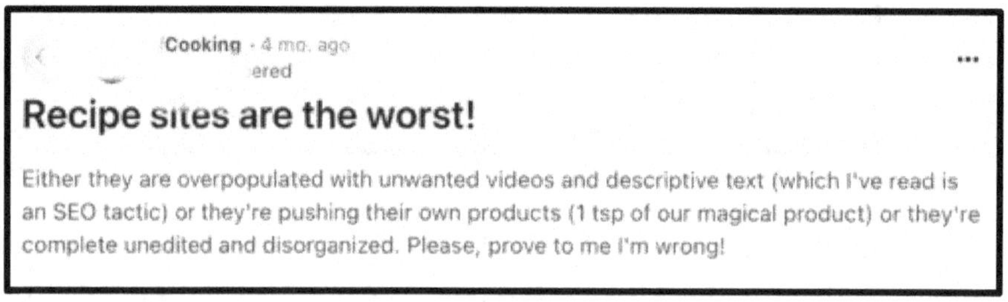

Look at this person too, they said if there isn't a "Jump to the recipe link" they are leaving, I felt like that about the pumpkin cheesecake recipe I was reading!

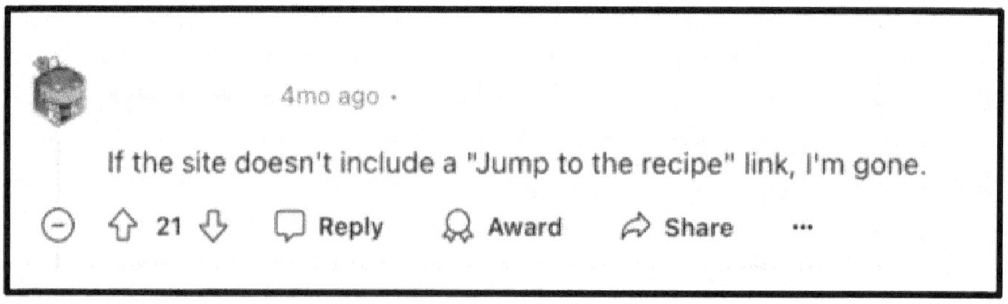

Now this example is just about recipe blogs but honestly, take my word for it, it is a problem across the internet. Don't be that blogger who is so focused on SEO tactics that you lose the human element of content creation.

Blogging should not be about just ranking on Google to get ad revenue, it should be about creating engaging pieces of writing that help and engage people.

Last Thoughts

So again, this is why when it comes to SEO content writing for beginners I recommend you only focus on using the basic SEO concepts like; "Keyword Researching", "On-Page SEO" and "Link-Building". And avoid tactics, gimmicks, "secret sauce", "mojo", and any of that other crap that does not work - just focus on writing content that your readers love, and more specifically you love!

If you focus on that first, higher rankings are a natural side effect. Now that you have an understanding of my SEO writing process and the SEO concepts that fuel it let's get into the first step, and that is how I go about finding a topic to write about.

Chapter 3: Finding Topics To Write About

When it comes to finding a topic to write about it is important that you choose ones that are "searchable" as in there are already articles out there on it, or at least you can find evidence that someone is interested in the topic you are writing about. As in, you can see a lot of people are searching for the topic with specific keywords or search terms.

It's okay to write about new ideas but at least some time should be spent on finding keywords or similar articles that are relevant to your topic idea. Now let's talk about why you should perform keyword research first.

Why Perform Keyword Research

There are a number of reasons to do keyword research first. For one, by performing proper **Keyword research**, beforehand, you can ensure that your articles are able to be found.

Don't be one of those newbs who avoids this step, this is the number 1 reason I see why new bloggers fail at getting more traffic; they don't take the time to research their topic beforehand. So before you start ask yourself these questions:

- What is the main topic of my article?
- What words or phrases do readers use to find similar articles like mine?
- What questions or problems is my article trying to address?
- What keywords do people type into search engines to find my topic?
- What other synonyms, acronyms, slang, or regional variations would people use to find similar articles like mine?

The point of asking yourself these questions is to get a sense of how your audience thinks, talks, and what they would be searching for, again this ensures that you are making content that is relevant and interesting to your audience, and also so you make the best use of your researching time. Now here's how to research:

So again think of keyword research not only as a way to find topics to blog about but also as a way to help you better gauge your own expertise, and whether or not you can ACTUALLY create the content.

Again guys the goal is to save money and time, but also to establish "Topical Authority" which is when readers and search engines start to see you as a credible source on a topic. Okay now that you started your keyword research let's go over how to pick the best ones.

How To Do Keyword Research

You might hear other SEO professionals talk about all these tools you can use and all these metrics you should follow like "search volume", "search intent" and "competition score", but it's really all about *relevancy*, as in choosing topics/keywords that people are actually searching for, and talking about.

Don't over-stress it. Using tools can be helpful but it's so easy to get caught up in choosing the "perfect keyword" that has the highest volume, or the lowest competition that you end up avoiding talking about critical topics that your unique readers want to hear your perspective on.

So again start with the basics. Once I have a topic in mind, I then do some minor keyword research just to make sure when I am writing I do not miss anything. The first thing I use is the *Auto-Suggest* feature of search engines.

Auto-Suggest

When just starting I recommend just using the *Auto-Suggest* feature of your preferred search engine. The auto-suggest feature is a tool on platforms like Google that shows users recommended keywords that may be related to what they are looking for. Let me give you an example. I typed in the keyword ***bread recipe***, as you can see in the screenshot below, Google recommended some different search terms:

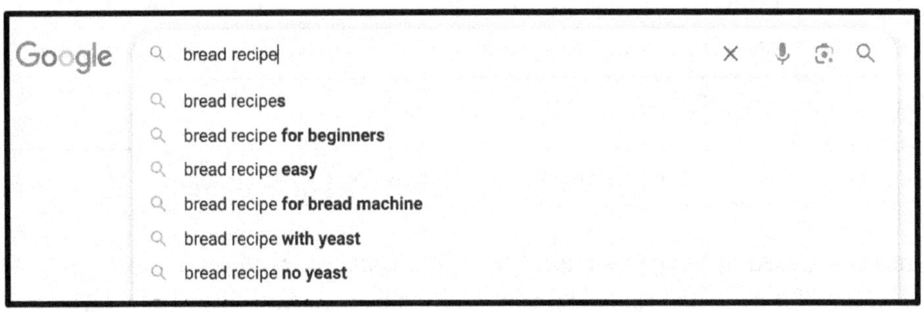

- *Bread recipes for beginners*
- *Bread recipe easy*

- *Bread recipe for bread machine*
- *Bread recipe with yeast*
- *Bread recipe no yeast*

Now these are all in theory their own unique recipes, but by using this auto-suggest feature you might see if there are some keywords that are also relevant to your content.

If my bread recipe also uses *active dry yeast, a bread machine*, and it's for *beginners* I should work these related terms into my recipe page somewhere. The point of doing this is to make your webpage more "relevant" and more "searchable".

Refer to Competitors

Another way to find relevant keywords is when in doubt just look at other bloggers who have similar articles; What I would do is make a list of similar articles to mine and then look to see what keywords they use. Check out this screenshot below from a blogger who made a bread recipe post:

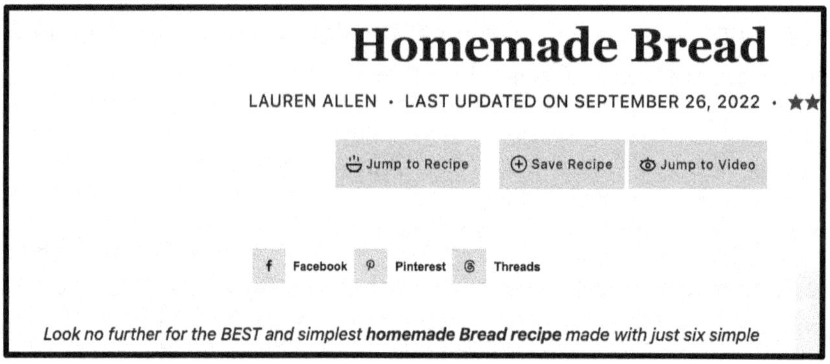

As you can see in the screenshot they mentioned, "homemade bread recipe". Mentioning "homemade" may be a good idea to use in my post if I was doing it. Hopefully, you can tell that by taking the time to research your competitors, you will be able to identify gaps in your own article and opportunities for new keywords to target.

Look At Forums and Message Boards

Forums and message boards are another great place to find blog ideas that maybe haven't been touched on yet. So they can be a good place to find article ideas. Also, they are a good place to find other relevant search terms that you might want to include in your writing. Check out the screenshot below from a forum poster, they want to know a sandwich loaf recipe.

That could easily be another new recipe to create, or I can take this keyword and apply it to my article if it is relevant. So again I would do the same thing, just look through the different forums, make a list of different topics, and choose the one that you feel is the best for you to write about or is the most applicable to your article.

Keyword Research Tools

Keyword research tools are usually my last afterthought because it's so easy to get caught up in all the graphs, and green lights, that you end up getting obsessive with a keyword. But they can be helpful if you need help with just finding more related search terms, but again I wouldn't lean on these tools for everything.

What To Do With Your Keywords

So with your keywords, I would write them down and keep them in a spreadsheet so you can easily refer to them as you write your content. You can see an example below in the screenshot. The spreadsheet doesn't have to be fancy, just functional.

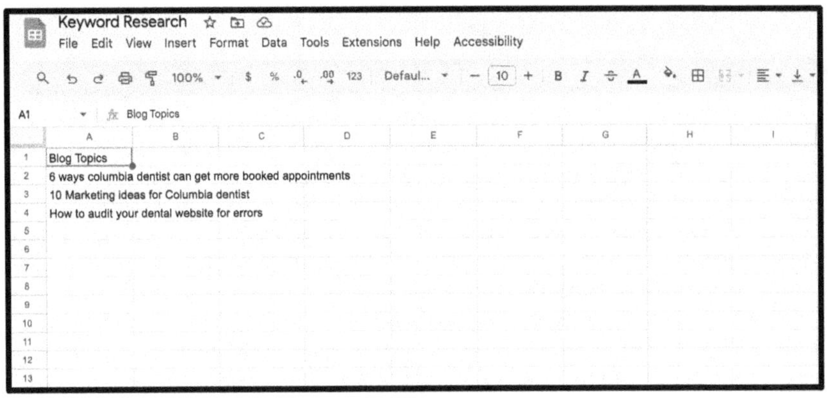

Last Thoughts

To close out this section, Keyword research should be more about finding relevant topics that people are already reading, rather than chasing the most viral topic you can find. Also, it's about finding other related terms that can help you better improve the searchability and semantics of your writing.

Again, keyword tools can be helpful but you should use them as a supplement, not as an end-all be-all. Okay so once you have a topic in mind, and some keywords it's time to start writing, let's go over how I would structure my SEO content.

Chapter 4: Structuring SEO Content

Hopefully, by now you have a solid blog topic idea with some related keywords that you want to write about. For the next step, you need to start actually writing your article, like I said earlier in Chapter 2, when it comes to writing SEO content and making it easier to read and understand for search engines you need to adhere to **On-Page SEO "**elements" like; **Title tags**, **Meta Descriptions**, and **Headings**. Here's some more additional detail on what they are:

- **Title Tag**: These tags function similarly to the title of a book or movie, as the tag provides a quick insight into the content and relevance of the webpage to a user's query. The title text is essential in enticing users to click on a result and providing them with valuable information.
- **Meta Description**: The Meta Description is the second piece of text a user encounters in each search result. Much like the title tag, its purpose is to captivate and persuade readers to visit your webpage by providing a quick summary of what the webpage is about.
- **Headers (H1, H2, H3, H4, H5, and H6)**: Headers are comparable to chapters found in a novel or book. Headers are used to help separate and identify ideas and paragraphs in web content. The usage of headers allows you to show your readers that they are going into more detail about a specific topic. Also, headers play a relevant role in search engines, as they assist them in better understanding the organization of your text on the page and evaluating its convenience for any searcher.

Additionally, you want to pay attention to web writing mechanics like the structure, formatting, and readability of your content like:

- **Keyword placement**: Making sure you use your keywords in your Title tag, Meta description, and throughout your article. Additionally, you can include keywords in your URL, to help with readability as well.
- **Paragraph Length**: Keeping paragraphs short and readable for a better user experience.
- **Bullet Points and Lists**: Breaking information into digestible formats to enhance readability.
- **Internal Links**: Linking to other relevant pages within the website to provide more context and improve SEO.

- **External Links**: Linking to other relevant websites/webpages on other sites that provide additional information or context.

- **Images:** Adding images can help with improving comprehension, additionally you can add *Image Alt Text* to help readers who are visually impaired and use screen reader software.

I hope that you were able to pick up from reading the suggestions, that the overall point of On-Page SEO is to make your writing more appropriate for a web format. Not so much to be picky about what you write or your unique writing style. These are not tactics, but instead just basic web etiquette.

Just imagine how hard it would be to read online if there weren't any titles, headings, or links, or if the writer didn't break up ideas with bullet points or short paragraphs. It would be frustrating as hell! So again, taking the time just to structure your article is critical to SEO success. Now let's discuss how to put these mechanics in practice.

How To Structure A Webpage

So when it comes to structuring your articles it's important to just focus on the basics. Let me give you an example to help you wrap your head around this. Below I included an example of an SEO piece of Content that I wrote for a made-up client's blog post:

Sample Page Copy

Keywords: Business credit, Business credit card guide, How to build business credit
URL: www.samsbanking.com/blog/**how-to-build-business-credit**.com

Title Tag
<title> **How to build business credit** in 5 steps | Sam's Banking </title>

Meta Description
<meta name="description" content=" **Building business credit** can help an entrepreneur grow their business, by building a credit history, and improving access to capital, here's how to do it." />

Headings
<h1> **How to build business credit** in 5 steps </h1>
<h2> What is **business credit?**</h2>
<h2> **1. Register your business** </h2>
<h2> **2. Register for a Dun & Bradstreet number** </h2>
<h2> **3. Apply for a business credit card** </h2>

<h2> **4. Register for relevant net 30 accounts** </h2>
<h2> **5. Pay all bills on time and avoid tax liens** </h2>
<h2> **How to maintain your credit** <h2>

So as you can see from the example, I first wrote the *keywords/topics* that my article is addressing - I do this to help with writing the actual article, which I'll show you in a second. Also, I structure out the URL, or the unique web address that my article is at, you see I again put the keyword in there too, again this helps with remembering the address for readers.

Next, I wrote a Title Tag, a Meta description, and I created Headings, for this example, there were only H1, and H2 headings used but, again H3 - H6 is available as well.

Now additionally, you may notice that I wrote the "tags" in a bit of a funky way with <, and >, /. This is how you write HTML (Hypertext markup language) which is the preferred way that a computer reads text - most blogging sites rarely have you write HTML yourself so don't worry about it for now, I am just showing it for context.

Lastly, once I have the basic On-Page SEO mechanics done, I then start writing my article, this is where the "web writing mechanics" come into play I mentioned like using bullet points and shorter paragraphs. This example is going to get quite long, so I am just going to show you with the first two paragraphs:

<h1> **How to build business credit** in 5 steps </h1>
Starting or growing a business often requires access to capital, and building strong business credit is a key step to making that happen. Business credit allows you to separate your personal finances from your business which makes it:

- Easier to secure loans
- Lower interest rates,
- Gain favorable payment terms with vendors.

Here's a beginner-friendly guide to help you **how to build business credit** in just five steps!

<h2> What is **business credit**?</h2>

Business credit is a track record of a business's financial responsibility, similar to personal credit for individuals. Lenders, suppliers, and financial institutions use your business credit to evaluate your company's ability to pay back loans and meet financial obligations.

A strong business credit score can open doors to various financing opportunities and better terms. It's vital because it allows you to obtain credit in the name of your business, without involving your personal credit, which minimizes personal financial risk.

Again looking at the example I showed, as you can see web writing mechanics were used. For the *keyword placement,* I bolded it to show what keywords were used, again paragraphs were deliberately kept short to help with skimming, and bullet points were added to help with digesting the information better.

Additionally to the example, we can add *Images*, *Internal* and *External links*. With images, it's important to remember that they should be "semantic" and not just decorative so for instance with the article:

<table>
<tr><th>Image 1</th><th>Image 2</th></tr>
<tr><td>

This is a better image:

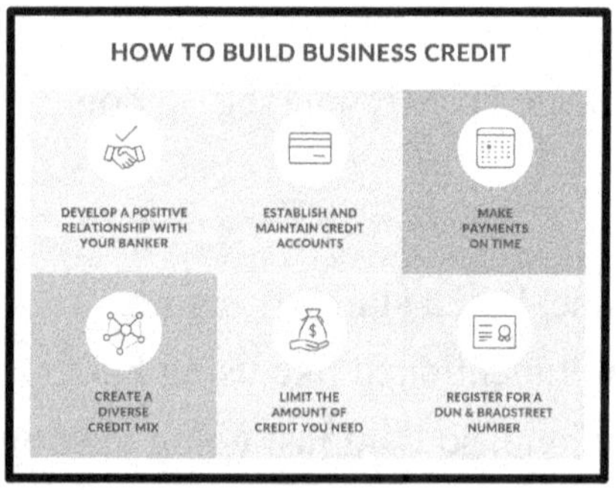

Cited from: https://www.johnsonfinancialgroup.com/resources/blogs/business-guidance/how-to-build-business-credit/

</td><td>

Then this image:

</td></tr>
</table>

The reason is Image 1, is more semantic it shows the steps that are being addressed in the article which again can help people who are skimming. While Image 2 is just decorative it doesn't necessarily communicate what the article is about - does this make sense?

For links, some good pages we could link to could be another related article on the same website about repairing business credit, so let's say the reader already has credit but it's in bad standing and they need help.

Another good link(s) could be links to some different banks that offer business credit. The "anchor text" or the clickable blue text that will be highlighted to show these links is below:

Hyperlinks

Add a hyperlink with anchor text "how to repair business credit" —-> https://www.samsbanking.com/how-repair-business-credit

Add a hyperlink with anchor text "banks that offer business credit" —-> https://www.banking.com/banks-offering-business-credit

As you can see I made the anchor text semantic as well, I included keywords to help with readability, this is another great tip - search engines dig this too! But like I echoed in Chapter 3, by showing you the recipe post example with the pumpkin cheesecake, you should not be spammy with the keywords.

Last Thoughts

That's the overall basics to writing a web article that is SEO-friendly and easy to read and comprehend for your audience. Now I am not going to go too much into detail on the overall mechanics of how I actually figure out what to write in the tags, and the content itself, as this is considered to be "copywriting" and that's for another book. But I will give you some just quick tips:

1. **Use of Power Words in Your Headlines**: Including emotionally charged or persuasive words that trigger interest and action.
2. **Add Call-To-Actions**: Writing direct and action-oriented CTAs to guide users toward desired actions (e.g., signing up, making a purchase, or clicking a link).
3. **Storytelling**: Engaging readers by telling a story or painting a picture that draws them in emotionally.
4. **Urgency and Scarcity**: Creating a sense of urgency (e.g., limited-time offers) to prompt action.
5. **Social Proof**: Using testimonials, case studies, or statistics to build credibility and persuade the audience.

All of these are not required, because they are more for marketing a product or a service, but they can be helpful tips for bloggers to help with promoting their own offers.

Okay so now let's get into the last step of my process which is how to get your content out there, and share it with relevant people.

Chapter 5: Sharing Your Content

Okay, so once you have a solid article written it is now time to get it out there, and promote it. When it comes to content creation this is yet another major mistake newbs make - they just think search engines are going to magically send traffic to the article.

Not a chance my friend! You have to start building up some credibility for the article. You can do this one way by getting what is called "backlinks", also known as editorial votes, and the process of getting these backlinks is called Link-building. Let me expand, backlinks essentially are instances where another website links or shares your article, and the reason this matters to search engines is because it makes the website owner seem more credible.

I think this is obvious though, obviously, you would be more swayed to read an article from someone who has been quoted and shared thousands of times versus someone who is new. But that's still not to say a beginner can't get traction. You just have to have a strategy and be patient.

How To Get Backlinks

So when it comes to getting your content out there and actually having someone share it, it really comes down to making sure you follow steps 1, and 2 of my process, and then finally start finding different website owners to share your content with. It's not rocket science. The main ways I use are:

- **Sending an email to relevant blog owners:** There's nothing wrong with sending a "cold email" to different blog owners in your niche and just seeing if they would share your article. Now I would actually take the time to get to know them first, or even offer payment but the key thing to remember is just be a regular human being, if your article is good, and you reach out to enough people there definitely will be one person who will link back to you. It's a start but not an end-all-be-all.
- **Using social media:** Another great way to get the word out about your blog posts is to create different social media accounts and share your posts on them. Now of course you need to make sure you are actually engaging with other people to build up a following, but once you do you may find that people will start to interact with you and share your content. Additionally, just ask people to do it, the worst they can say is no, or just not respond.

- **Guest Blogging:** Reaching out to blog owners and asking to collaborate or do a guest post is a great way to get the word out about you as a blogger in general. Additionally, it can help with getting your post found, in your guest post you can link up your previous post so that more people can see them.

Avoid Rushing The Process

Now again, I know what you are thinking - "Is that all I can do?". Unfortunately yes, there isn't a secret method to just getting a bunch of backlinks - well there are methods, but they will do WAY more harm than good.

This is why I recommend to new bloggers that patience is key. If you feel like your articles are great, don't wait for search engines or people to find you, hit the ground running and share your content around!

But whatever you shouldn't do, do not try to rush things by buying any of those backlink packages you see on freelancer sites. These backlinks are considered to be spam by search engines, so this can get your website removed from results. So again, buyer beware!

Last Thoughts

I know that a lot of people who read this book may have been expecting me to go into ravishing details about all the ways to build links, but honestly, I don't think they matter.

I think what's more important is having amazing content, and then taking the time to let other website owners know about it. But, I am certainly not one of those SEO professionals that says; *"just make good content, and people will find it on their own"*.

The key thing to take away from this step is that; you have to be able to persuade a website owner to want to link back to you. This doesn't happen overnight. You have to build relationships with these website owners naturally.

My best advice is to start with creating content that is of value, and then reach out to website owners to give it an extra boost. In other words, there is not a conveyor belt-like method to getting backlinks, it takes time and consistency. Okay, there you have it, that is my 3 step process for making SEO content, let's get into the last chapter.

Chapter 6: Last Words

As you can see, the SEO writing process can be very simple if you make it so. For a beginning blogger, I think this is more than enough information to help you get started with creating content that is enjoyable but also searchable.

With doing SEO it is very important to take care of all of the important mechanics and attention to detail beforehand because as I have been echoing throughout the book, SEO is a long game. So the longer it takes to implement sound suggestions, that are rooted in conceptualization and not tactics, the longer it may take to see results that you want.

My hope for you is that you will take your time and actually enjoy the journey of becoming a blogger. I would be a fool to say that I don't know that there are people who picked up this book just because they think or heard someone say that blogging online is a fast way to make money. Maybe in 2008, but in this time and age, blogging is strictly about showcasing expert opinions from actual professionals.

Blogging has become too much about chasing virality, that there are so many pseudo-experts running around on the internet, trying to get as many people to read their content as possible by writing about what they think sounds good, and not necessarily rooted in any real knowledge or research.

The truth is too many entry-level bloggers, and even digital marketing agencies do this, they make the mistake of trying to mimic or pretend that they know a subject just so they can create content for it.

Like I said earlier in Chapter 1, about search engines not being archaic anymore, in other words, they know if you do not know what the hell you are talking about or if you are just virtue signaling - and so can readers!

This is why it is so important to know your lane. If you do not know a topic it is worth the time and money to consult with someone who is in that field and knows the vernacular and the nuances of their industry.

This will help you make better content that is not only more credible but something readers can respect more. Also only make content that readers will find value in, not just content that you think might get the highest ranking.

For instance, if you are a food blogger don't spend your time trying to chase every viral recipe, instead focus on creating content for recipes that you know how to make first, and then later down the road as you get feedback on your content you will discover other content ideas that are worth exploring.

Here's another example, if you are a journalist focusing on writing articles on current events is always a good place to start, but do your research first to see if it's a topic that you can actually speak on. When creating content you should never want to share misinformation, again this is why it is so important to consult industry experts for content creation.

Let me give you one more thorough example, marketing agencies, for instance, love to sell these "content packages" - as in give you, for say 5 or 10 blogs a month, or something like that for a flat fee. Also, these agencies tend to work with professionals like doctors, home improvement professionals, lawyers, etc.

As you can imagine someone in each of these professions must have to know a lot of jargon to complete their work. So here's where agencies make this mistake - because they are so focused on selling their "packages" they do this almost pump-and-dump process where they rapidly produce content (think AI), but the content lacks:

- Originality
- Variance
- Semantics
- Attitude
- Expert opinion

Basically, it sounds like a bot did it, but it's not always a bot. Sometimes it's a freelancer, on one of those five-dollar websites…who used a bot themselves. What I am trying to say is when it comes to content creation you should take your time to make sure it's actually enjoyable.

If you do that, you will find that it really doesn't matter how viral, or high your rankings are. What you instead will find is that having a small well engaged following that actually purchases your products, and attentively consumes your content is what it is all about. So again, use SEO as the fuel to make this happen but don't stress about it.

Hopefully, this book encourages you to really take your time and enjoy being a blogger, doing this will make sure you have a more fruitful experience with creating content. Thanks for reading, and see you next time!

About the Author

Roggie (Raj) Clark, is a 9-year SEO professional and owner of the SEO agency; *Bounce Rank.* Prior to joining the SEO industry, Raj was a web developer and school teacher. It was through creating his own websites, and wanting a career change from teaching, that Raj stumbled across the world of SEO.

Since joining the field nearly a decade ago, Raj has worked on a wide range of campaigns, from eCommerce to B2B, to Healthcare, for enterprise companies and marketing agencies in the United States.

He is regarded as an expert, and guru by his colleagues, and the SEO industry. Raj currently lives in Odenton, Maryland with his sister and niece.

Learn HTML, CSS, and JavaScript With This One Book

The **Basics of Front-End Web Development (HTML, CSS, and JavasScript)**. To learn all three coding languages, check out the full book.

https://www.amazon.com/Basics-Front-End-Development-HTML-JavaScript-ebook/dp/B0DJ147B15

Learn SEO

Learning SEO ensures that visitors can actually find your website and apps on the internet. Below I included links to several SEO books I've written. They are excellent reads.

The ABCs of SEO: Search Engine Optimization 101

https://www.amazon.com/ABCs-Search-Engine-Optimization-Page-ebook/dp/B0C2JSLW7M

The Technical SEO Handbook

https://www.amazon.com/Technical-SEO-Handbook-Learn-Issues-ebook/dp/B0CMBJR9QV

Creating An SEO Strategy 101

https://www.amazon.com/Creating-SEO-Strategy-101-Link-Building-ebook/dp/B0D92YJZ2N

Consulting Or Coaching Services

I know that from reading this book, it simply may not be enough information for you or you may require more personalized support with your unique business situation.

So because of that, I'm offering the opportunity to receive consulting or coaching from me on SEO. I can offer support with:

- Creating SOPs (Standard Operating Procedures)
- Creating SEO strategies
- SEO Implementation
- Content Suggestions
- Technical Audits
- Web design/migrations
- Competitor analysis
- Keyword research
- SEO Career Coaching

If you are interested in any of these services or would like to request more information, for a specific need you may have.

Please email me at bouncerankseo@gmail.com. In your email, please include the following information:

- Your name
- The business you represent (if applicable)
- Team size (if applicable)
- The length of service needed
- Any other important information I should know

My administrative assistant will email you back within 24 - 48 hours with rates, and an information sheet for you to review. Thank you so much for your time and interest.

www.ingramcontent.com/pod-product-compliance
Lightning Source LLC
LaVergne TN
LVHW080002210926
848481LV00012B/3651